THIS BOOK BELONGS
TO

TEST YOUR COLORS HERE

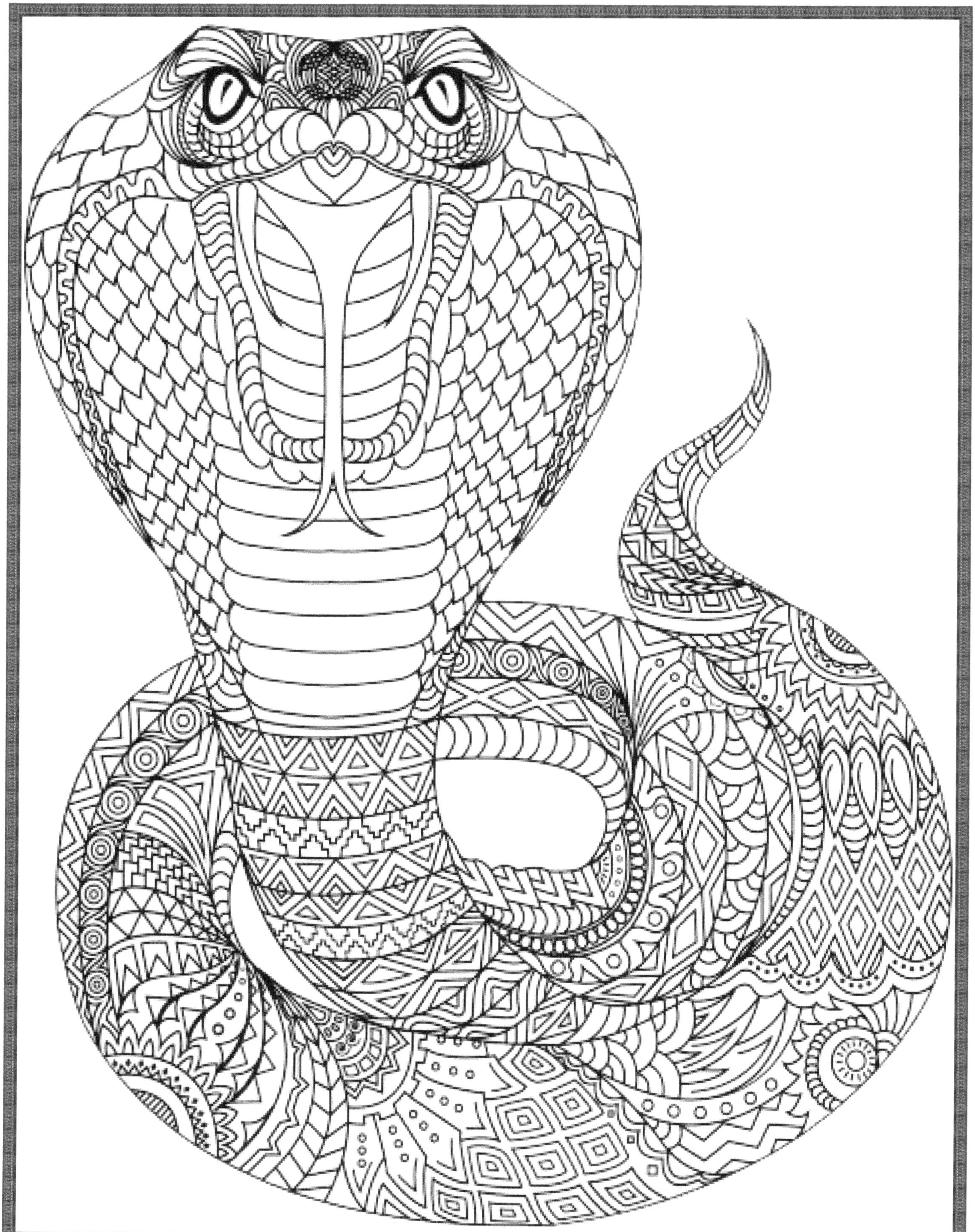

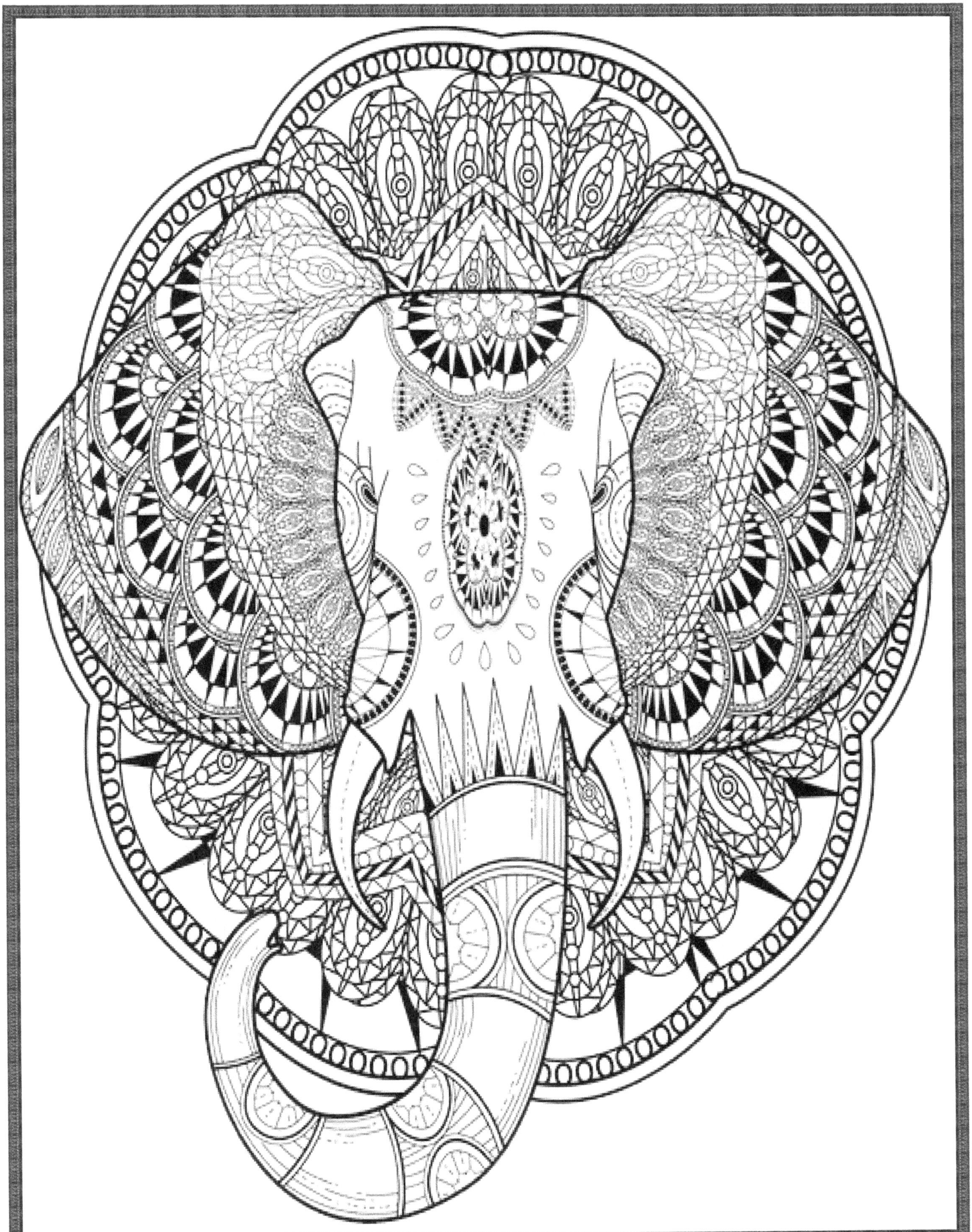

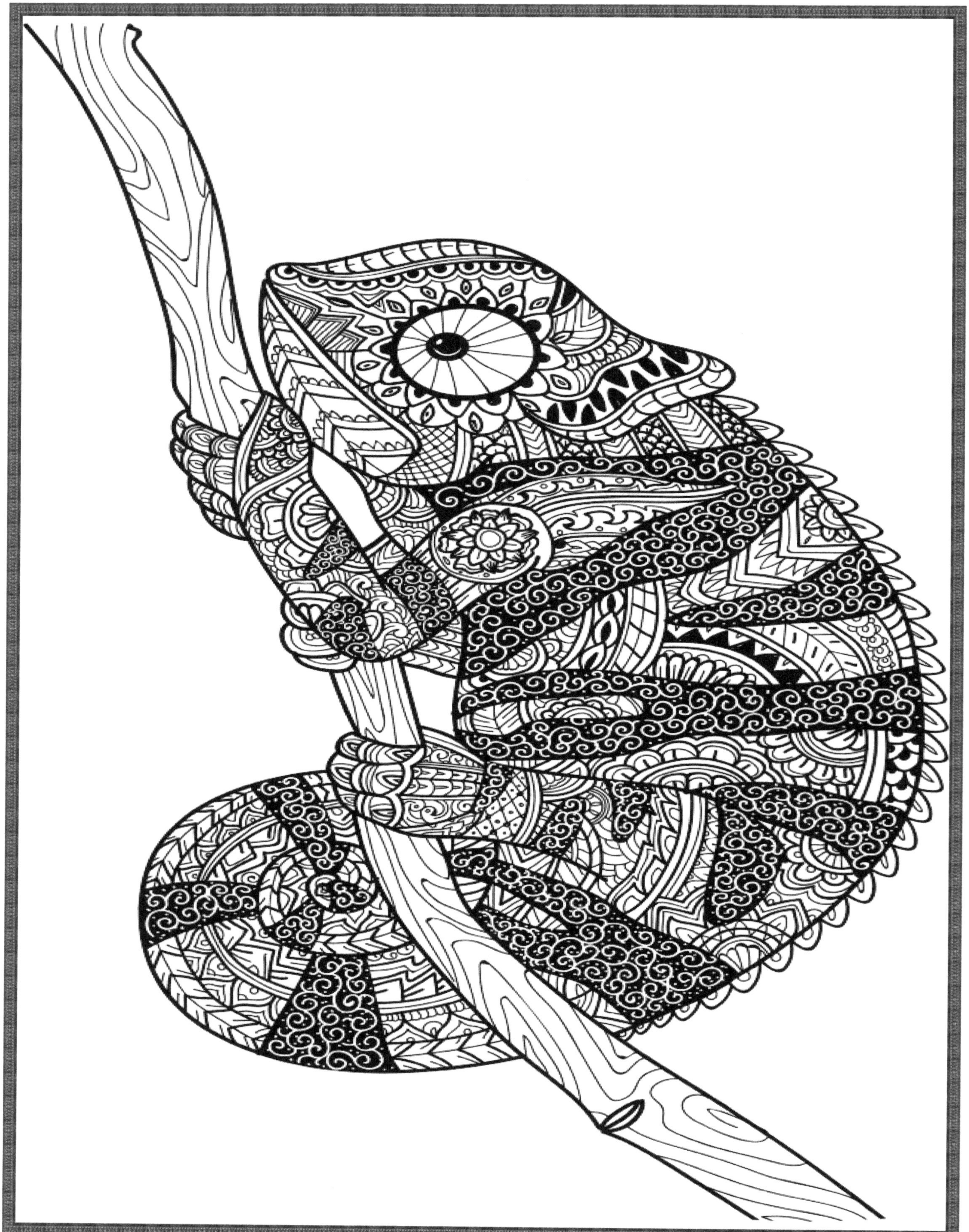

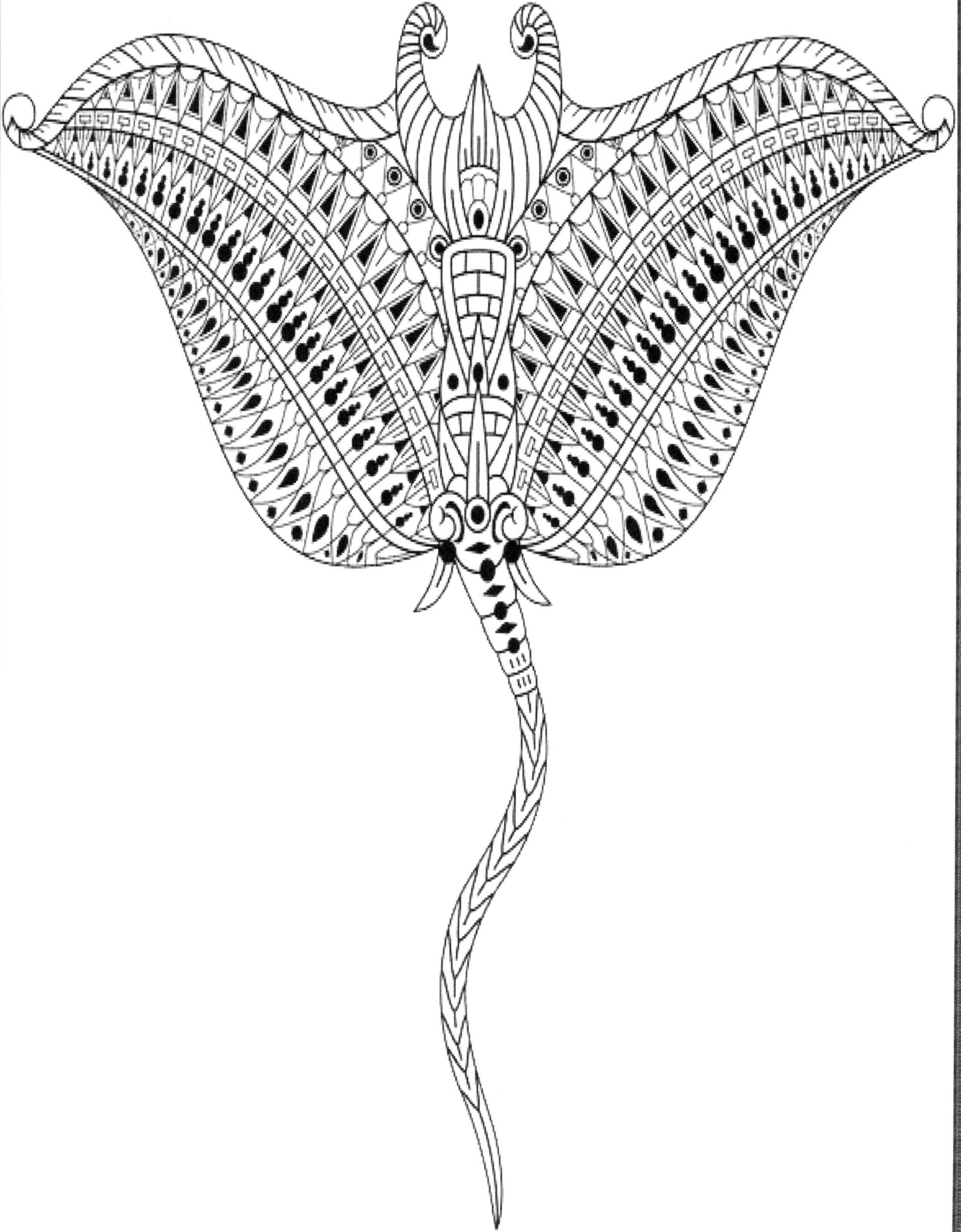

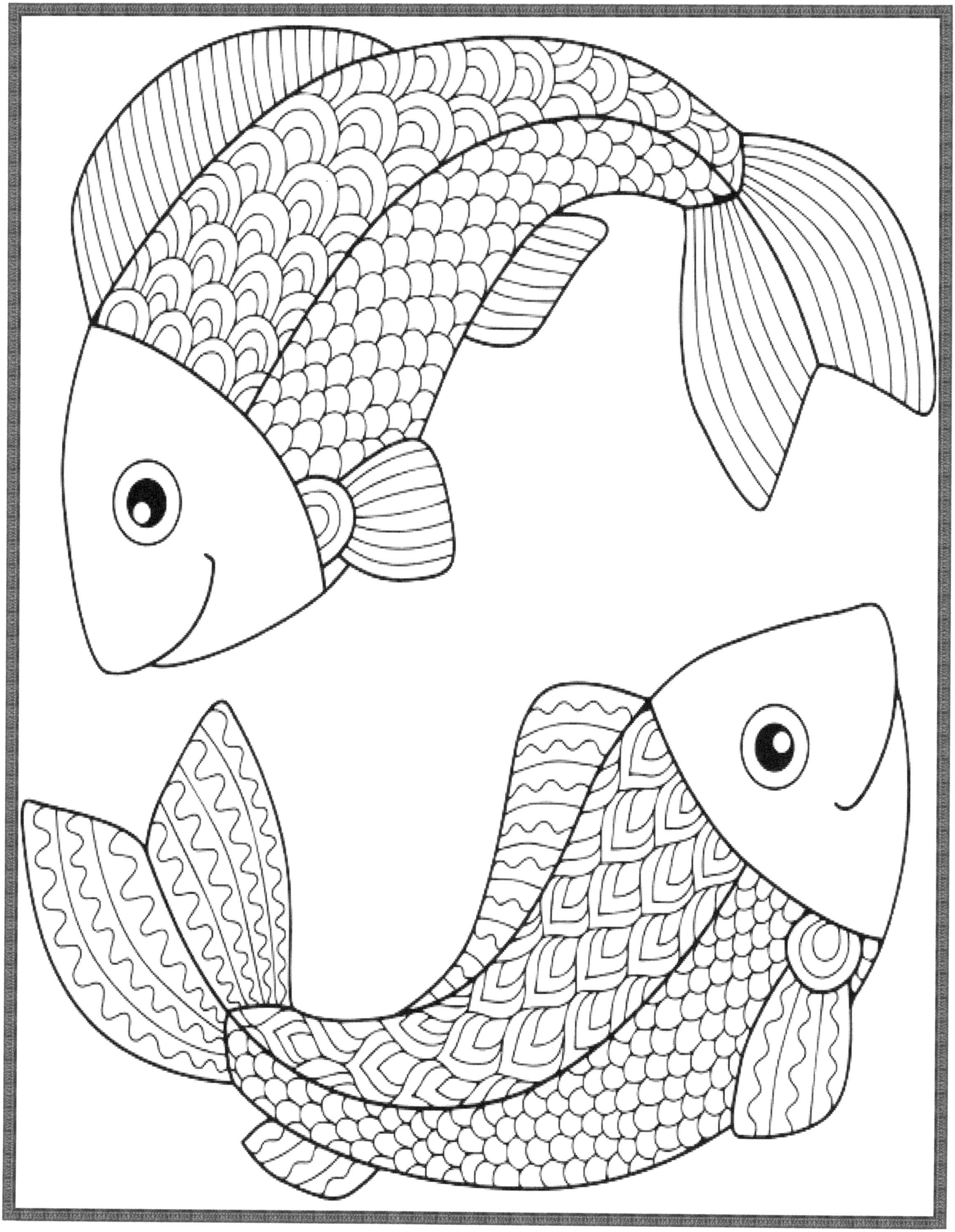

OC

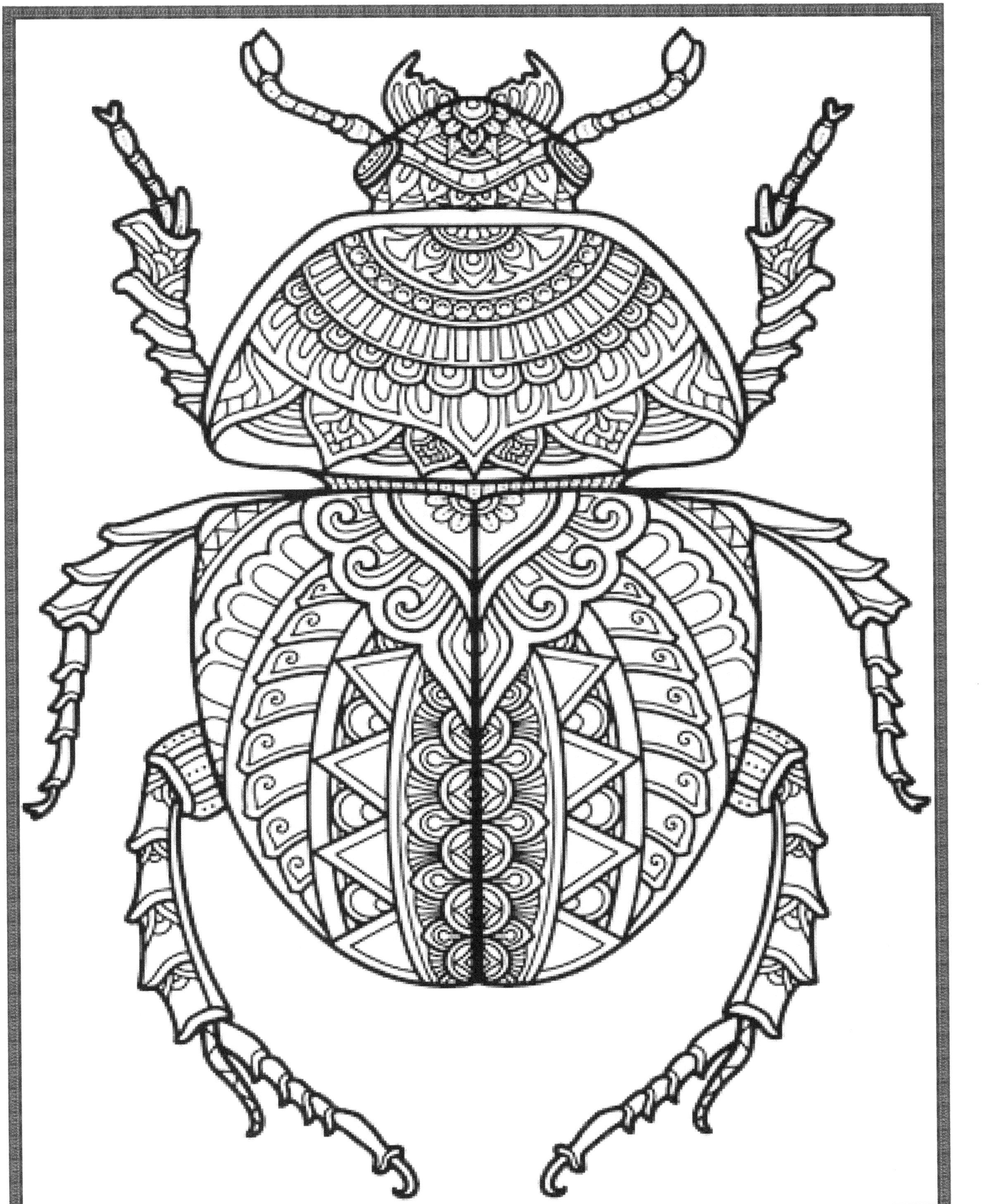

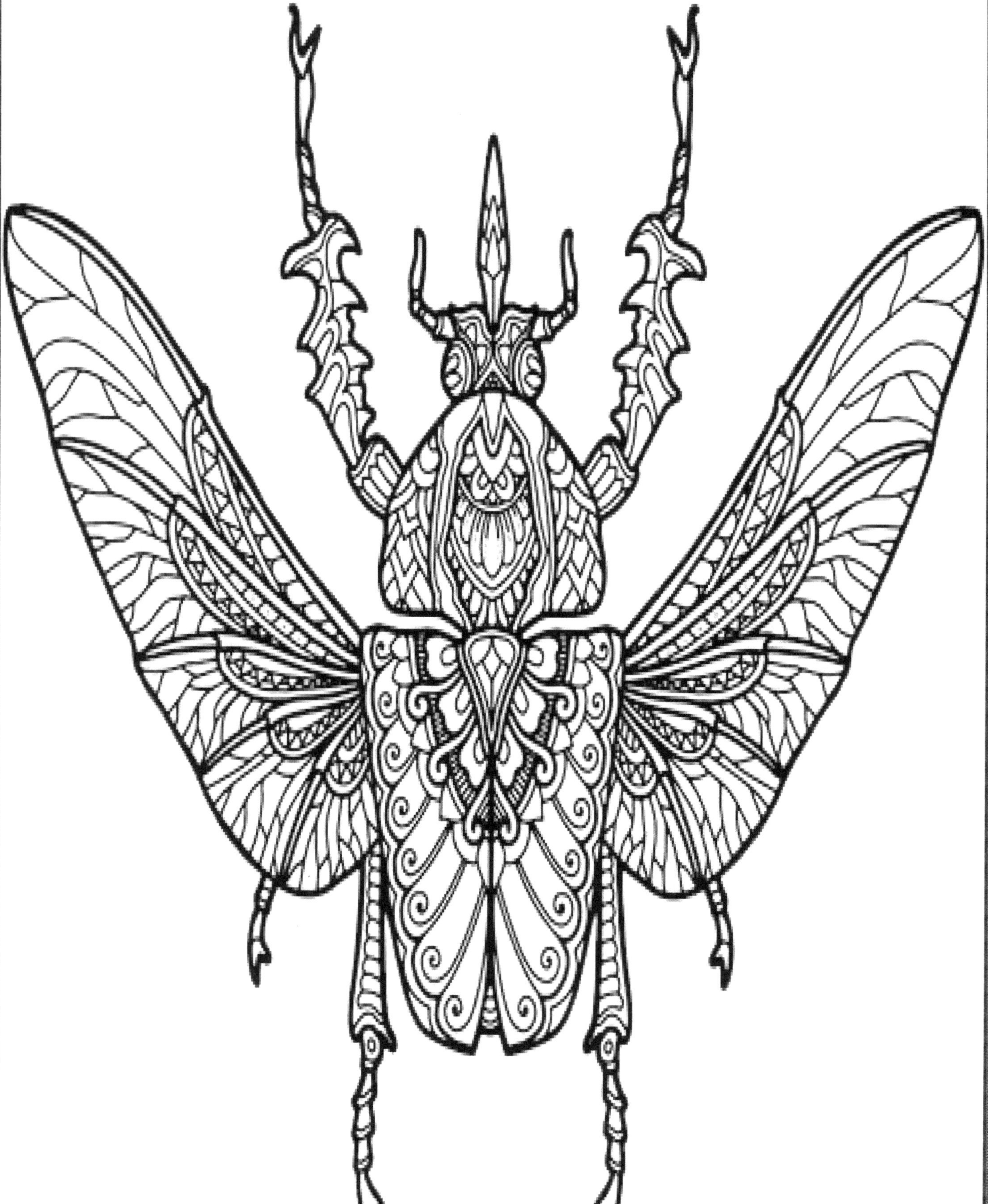

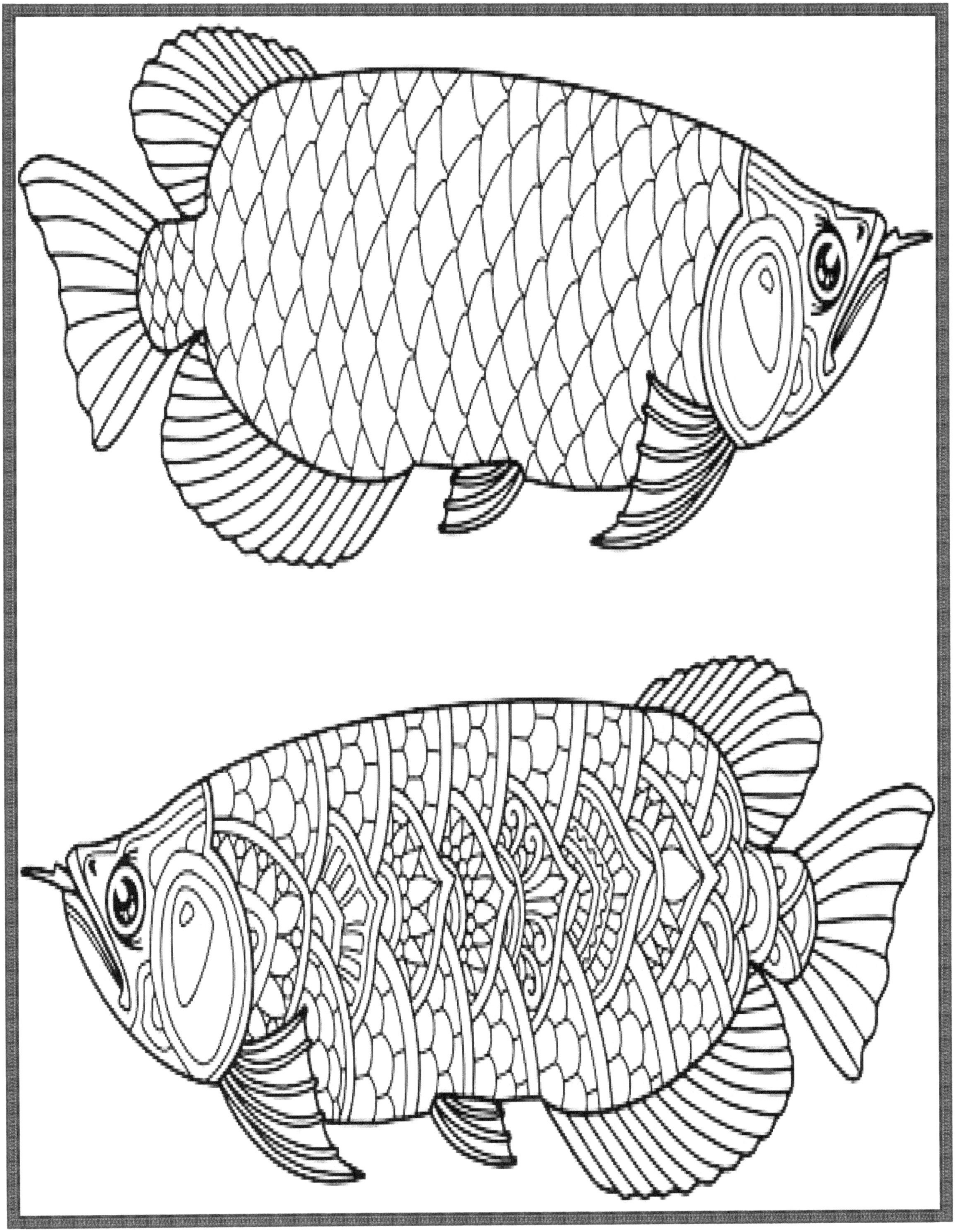

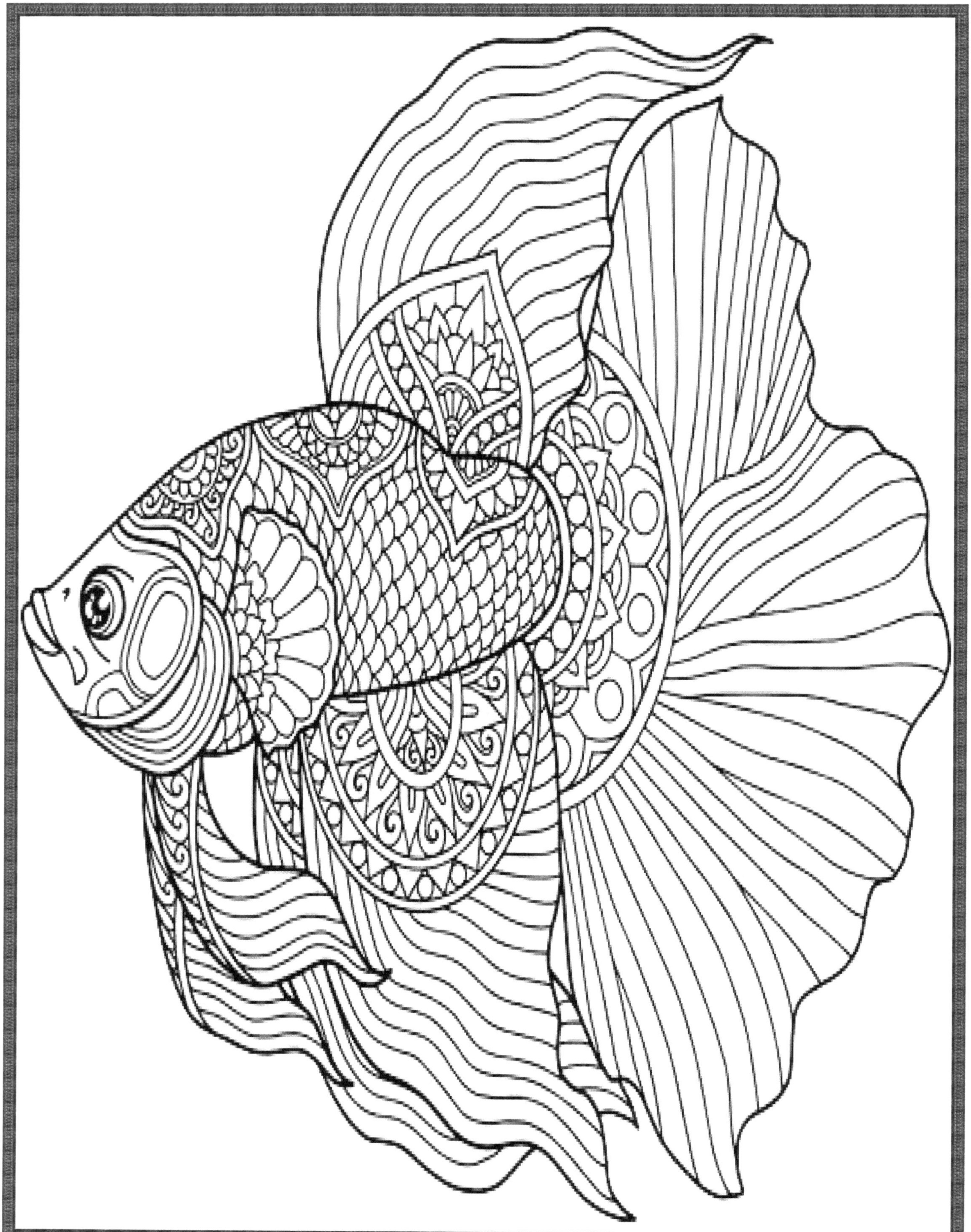

www.ingramcontent.com/pod-product-compliance
Lightning Source LLC
Chambersburg PA
CBHW081718231224
19440CB00031B/570

9 798672 707730